CW01558632

Trial by 1

Quick and Easy Medieval Wargames Rules

Written By Mark Lord

Website: https://marklord.info/trial-by-battle/

Contents

3

Introduction

What is a Wargame?

Wargames can take many forms. For many if you say wargame they might think of military exercises, with real soldiers and tanks roaming across the countryside shooting each other with blanks, for others a wargame is a boardgame that involves hexes and counters, or a computer game involving 3d digital tanks and soldiers. What you have here though are the rules for playing what might more accurately be called a tabletop miniatures wargame where players fight each other using armies of miniature soldiers. Wargames of this sort are played on a table with terrain representing the field of battle and with plastic or metal soldiers grouped into units on bases. Dice are thrown to determine the results of combat between the armies and each player tries to outwit the other to win the game. Wargames are played with numerous sets of rules and types of game. There's no set standard size game like there maybe with a boardgame. You can play with as many or as few miniature soldiers as you like.

About these Rules

Trial by Battle is a set of wargames rules for playing games set in the Medieval period of history. They are designed to be really easy to learn and to play and are ideal for a quick game, especially with players who are not very familiar with wargames rules and who want a simple game. Sometimes this type of ruleset is called a "beer and pretzels" game. Neither beer nor pretzels are required to play, but a game is always more enjoyable with good refreshments.

The rules aim to be representative of how medieval armies fought but aren't an exact simulation and don't provide for all the different variations in types of soldiers and armies during the Medieval period. For instance, the Archers unit could represent crossbowmen or longbowmen. The rules should provide the framework for an enjoyable Medieval wargame that captures the feel of battles in the Middle Ages.

To help get you started playing medieval wargames using Trial of Battle, I have provided six scenarios that could take place between any armies. Each battle in these scenarios uses roughly 6 to 8 units per side. There are also some sample army lists provided for different armies of the Medieval period.

What you need to play

To play Trial by Battle you will need:

A table - a standard kitchen table will be enough. Anything that is at least 3' x 3' is adequate, but if you want to fight bigger battles with more miniatures then more space would be ideal. All the scenarios in this book are designed for a 3' x 3' space, which should fit comfortably onto a standard kitchen table.

Miniatures - you will need miniature figures or paper soldiers to play your battles. These can be of any scale. Scales for wargames range from as small as 2mm high to 54mm, but the most common scales tend to be 6mm, 10mm, 15mm and 28mm. Numerous manufacturers and suppliers of miniature figures can be found on the internet.

Basing - miniatures can be based in any way you prefer. I would recommend that unit frontages are no more than 4" or 5" so that you can fit units on a 3' x 3' table, however, you could use smaller or bigger bases depending on the table space available to you. I tend to use units of ten 28mm miniatures for infantry arranged in two ranks of five. Each miniature is on a 20mm x 20mm base which gives a unit frontage of 100mm or about 4". For cavalry I have a unit of four on bases 25mm by 50mm which again gives the same 100mm frontage. But that's just my preference and is not a "rule"!

Terrain - it's possible to buy or make some wonderful wargames terrain, but if just starting out you could use card made buildings, toy buildings or even Lego to make terrain. The classic old-school way of making hills is to put books under a green cloth, and that still works for a lot of people.

Dice - a number of six-sided dice to play the game. I would recommend about 10 dice would be useful. I refer to these as d6 in the book. 1d6 means roll one dice, 2d6 means roll two dice and add the results together.

A tape measure or ruler in inches - for measuring movement and archery ranges.

An opponent or solo - it's always most fun to play a wargame against an opponent, but that's not always possible. You can always play against yourself - simply take the role of both generals and see what happens! If you want to add complexity you can dice to see what each general would do in different situations, add chance cards etc. There are some books available on solo wargaming, and I have a post on my blog detailing some of these.

Armies in Trial by Battle

In a standard game of Trial by Battle armies are formed of six units lead by a general. Larger and smaller armies can be used depending on the scenario. Army lists are also provided later in this book to give you an idea of what units an army should contain.

In Trial by Battle soldiers are formed into units categorized as one of six different types.

Mounted Knights

This unit type covers all heavy cavalry in the period who would use the impetus of their charge to sweep away their enemies. Usually well armoured and using a lance at first contact, mounted knights were most effective when they first charged an enemy. Therefore, in Trial by Battle they do more hits on their first melee phase in a battle. Against lesser opponents this should be enough to win the first round of combat and after that the momentum of the impact should see them as winners. Although their mounted state helped get them across the battlefield and added to the force of their initial charge, horses also represented a large target for archers and could be surrounded by infantry after the initial charge. Therefore, mounted knights do not get the highest Saving Throw in the game, but at 4+ it's still good.

Light Cavalry

This unit covers all light cavalry that was meant for skirmishing or harassing the enemy with archery. Think Mamluk horse archers and Mongolian cavalry here. They are fast and can maneuver better than other units apart from light infantry, but they are weak in melee and their archery is less effective than formed units of foot Archers.

Foot Knights

Representing dismounted knights using polearms such as those deployed by the English and later by the French in the Hundred Years War but could also include well-motivated bodies of heavy infantry such as Flemish pikemen that would not break easily. They have the best saving throw in the game at 3+ partly because of their armour, but also because of their courage and motivation. They will often form the core of a tough infantry based medieval army.

Infantry

Infantry units cover units of spearmen, billmen and militia. They will usually be fairly well-armoured with helmets, mail coats and maybe a shield, and armed with spears or polearms. They are not very well-trained, being composed of the retainer of noble households or town militiamen, so not as effective in battle as knights or more motivated heavy infantry. They are armoured though and form compact bodies of troops, so get a Saving Throw of 4+.

Archers

Archers are any group of foot soldiers armed with bows such as longbows or crossbows. They will usually be less well armoured than infantry or foot knights and be in a looser formation. It could be argued that crossbowmen protected by pavises should be treated differently, but for the purposes of these quick and easy rules I have chosen to make them the same as other archers as the battlefield role and effectiveness would be about the same.

Light Infantry

Groups of more irregular infantry, lighter armed and with less discipline than other units. They can as a result move faster than other infantry but are weak in combat. They are useful in areas of rough terrain. Welsh spearmen and French ribalds would be examples of Light Infantry.

The Rules

Units

Units in Trial by Battle are split into six types:

- Mounted Knights
- Light Cavalry
- Foot Knights
- Infantry
- Archers
- Light Infantry

A figure should also be included to represent the leader of the army - the General. The General can provide modifiers to Units and is used when making Army Courage Tests to determine if the army breaks or not.

Unit Name	Move	Archery Hits	Range	Melee Hits	Save	Stamina
Mounted Knights	9"	n/a	n/a	1d6+1/1d6	4+	6
Light Cavalry	12"	1d6-2	12"	1d6-2	6+	6
Foot Knights	4"	n/a	n/a	1d6	3+	6
Infantry	6"	n/a	n/a	1d6-1	4+	6
Archers	6"	1d6-1	18"	1d6-2	5+	6
Light Infantry	9"	n/a	n/a	1d6-2	6+	6
General	12"	n/a	n/a	+1	n/a	n/a

Rounds, Phases and Priority

The game is split into rounds. In each round there are three phases:

- Movement - units can move
- Archery - Light Cavalry and Archers can shoot ranged weapons
- Melee - units engaged in hand-to-hand combat must fight

At the start of the battle priority is determined either through the specific rules written in the scenario or by each player rolling 1d6 and the player with the highest score choosing to go either first or second in each phase. If both players roll the same number, then roll again until there is not a tie.

The player with priority will then go first in the Movement and Archery phases of the battle. The player without priority goes second in those phases. Fighting in the Melee phase is always simultaneous. Even if a unit is broken it still gets a chance to roll for hits against the units it is fighting.

Movement

Each Unit can move up to the distances below in their turn:

Light Cavalry	12"
Mounted Knights	9"
Light Infantry	9"
Foot Knights	4"
Infantry and Archers	6"
General	12"

Most units can turn up to 45 degrees without a movement penalty. If they turn 90 degrees, they can only move up to half their movement allowance. If they turn 180 degrees, they cannot move.

Light Cavalry and Light Infantry suffer no movement penalty for turning.

Units can turn at any point during movement. However, if wishing to engage enemy in the melee phase the turn must be at the start of the movement phase. It is possible to turn 90 degrees and still charge. An unengaged Unit that is attacked in front or rear will turn to face automatically.

Terrain Effects:

Only Light Infantry and Cavalry can move through woods. They do so at half their normal movement allowance.

Other difficult terrain such as swamps, broken ground, muddy fields, obstacles such as ditches, walls and hedges reduce movement by half. If more than one of these is combined, then movement would be a quarter. For instance, an infantry unit (move 6") moving through a muddy field that then needs to cross a ditch, would have movement halved to 3" by the muddy field and then halved again to cross the ditch. So, they could only move one and a half inches towards the ditch and then cross the next turn.

Streams and rivers may be fordable with a penalty cost of half movement. It should be agreed before the battle if streams and rivers can be forded and where along their length.

Archery

Archers have a range of 18" and cannot move and shoot. The target must be in front of the Archer unit in a 90-degree arc.

Light Cavalry has a range of 12" and can move and shoot or shoot and move. They can shoot in any direction.

Shooting Units choose one enemy Unit to fire against. This should be the closest Unit to them that they can fire at - i.e., in their front arc for Archers.

Archery and fighting in Melee result in enemy Units possibly losing Stamina through Hits. To determine the number of Hits each Unit makes against an enemy Unit a 1d6 is rolled and modified as follows:

Archers roll 1d6-1

Light Cavalry roll 1d6-2

The Unit targeted by archery then makes a Saving Throw for each hit against it. Each type of Unit has a different Save as follows:

Mounted Knights 4+

Foot Knights 3+

Infantry 4+

Archers 5+

Light Cavalry 6+

Light Infantry 6+

If the target unit is in cover such as woods, behind a wall or hedge then they get +1 to their saving throw. For instance, Infantry behind a hedge would have a save of 3+, while Light Infantry in woods would have 5+.

For each hit against the unit, it makes a roll on a d6 and must score equal or over their Save to negate the hit. Hits will accumulate from round to round, so they need to be recorded in some way. Unsaved Hits are recorded using any of several different methods, for example a token, a dice, removal of figures from a movement tray or marking against the unit in a roster as preferred.

When a Unit takes six Hits their Stamina is reduced to zero and they will need to make a Unit Courage Test. See the section after the Melee for details of this Test.

Melee

As in the Archery Phase Units roll to see how many Hits they inflict, and the opposing unit makes a Saving Throw to prevent loss of Stamina. However, in the Melee phase both units engaged roll to Hit. Hits are simultaneous, so if a unit is Broken because of a failed Unit Courage Test it will still roll for Hits against its enemy.

Hits are modified differently to those in the Archery Phase:

Mounted Knights 1d6+1 on first Melee Phase they engage in during the Battle. Thereafter 1d6 Hits

Foot Knights 1d6

Infantry 1d6-1

Archers, Light Infantry and Light Cavalry 1d6-2

Also, units receive +1 if they are on a hill above the enemy unit they are fighting. Also +1 if the enemy unit recoiled in the Melee Phase in the last round. If a general is with the unit, they also add +1 to the Hit roll.

Saving Throws are the same as for Archery:

Mounted Knights 4+

Foot Knights 3+

Infantry 4+

Archers 5+

Light Cavalry 6+

Light Infantry 6+

There is no +1 Save for Cover, but there is +1 Save for Infantry and Foot Knights flanked by other Infantry or Foot Knights to represent the benefit of massed close order infantry or a shield wall formation.

If a unit is already engaged to its front and then attacked in the flank or rear then it must split its Hits between the enemy units as equally as possible, but if the Hits result is an odd number, then allocate more to the unit in front. For instance, on a roll of 3 it would split 2 to the front and 1 to the enemy on the flank.

At the end of the Melee phase the winner of the fight between two units is determined by which side inflicted the most unsaved Hits. If no Hits are suffered or the number of Hits that phase is equal, then it is a draw. If there is a winner, then the loser recoils 2" and the winner follows up. If the loser is a mounted unit versus an infantry unit, then they can break off and make a full move away. The mounted unit spends the next Round reforming and may not move or shoot.

The winner of the fight receives a +1 to Hit rolls next Round.

For melee combats involving several units the total Hits are added together and the recoil is for the whole group. For example, a single unit of Foot Knights is in Melee against a unit of Infantry to its front and Light Cavalry to its flank. The Foot Knights inflict 5 Hits in total, 3 on the Infantry, and 2 on the Light Cavalry. The Infantry and Light Cavalry together only manage 3 Hits on the Foot Knights, so both the Infantry and Light Cavalry recoil. They will recoil in the direction of the front facing enemy and the Light Cavalry will remain in contact on the flank.

When a Unit takes six Hits their Stamina is reduced to zero and they will need to make a Unit Courage Test.

Unit Courage Test

Once 6 Hits have been taken by the unit in total, they make a Unit Courage Test. Roll 2d6 and if the result is 7 or less then the Unit passes and can continue. Over 7 and the unit Breaks. It is removed from the table.

If a Unit passes and remains on the table, it must make another Unit Courage Test whenever it suffers more Hits.

Winning and Losing

Once an army loses half or more of its Units it must make an Army Courage Test by rolling 2d6. If the General is still alive and not captured, then the player must roll or 8 or less for the army to keep fighting. A roll of more than 8 means that the whole army has lost heart and concedes the battle.

It is possible for both armies to fail an Army Courage Test at the same time in which case the Battle is a draw.

If the General has been killed or captured, then the player must roll 6 or less to pass an Army Courage Test.

The General

The army's General can join a unit and add +1 to their Hits in Melee and also remove 3 hits suffered by the Unit. Removing hits can happen when the general joins the unit or later. Removing hits can only be done once during a battle and only for one unit. Also, if the Unit needs to make a Unit Courage Test this is passed on a roll of 8 or less instead of 7.

But if the unit the general has joined is destroyed the general will be killed or captured. On a roll of 1-3 the general is dead on a roll of 4-6 they are captured. This may have significance if playing a campaign.

General moves 12" a turn. Cannot be shot or killed if not with a unit. Once with a unit the general cannot leave it for rest of the battle.

Scenarios

A standard battle can be fought using two armies and by fighting until one or both armies have failed an Army Courage Test. The battlefield can be determined either by mutual agreement or randomly. If randomly for each 1-foot square roll a dice. On a 1 to 4 that part of the battlefield is empty on a 5 or 6 it contains a terrain feature. Roll again on the following table:

Dice Roll	Terrain Feature
1-2	Hill
3	Swamp/Marsh or other rough ground - rocky ground if arid location
4	Field enclosed by hedges or walls
5-6	Wood

If you want to play a different type of battle, you can either base a scenario on an historical battle or come up with an imaginary scenario. Over the next few pages are a selection of six scenarios that can be used to spice up your battles. Some of these include specific terrain and all include a suggested map of the battlefield. However, you can equally choose your own terrain or determine it randomly using the table above.

The six scenarios presented here are:

1. Meeting Engagement
2. Flank Attack
3. Last Stand
4. Ambush
5. Rear Guard

6.   River Crossing

Sometimes to distinguish between them the armies are labelled Red or Blue - simply switch these names with the names of your armies for each scenario.

Notes on the Maps

Each map is based on a 3' by 3' table. Grids have been provided at 1' intervals. You can adjust the map size to your own table set-up.

Meeting Engagement

Two opposing armies have been drawing closer to each other over a period of days and have finally encountered each other. There is no time to draw up battle lines in a set piece battle, so each army must handle the deployment of its forces as best it can.

Objectives

The objective for both armies is the same, to defeat the other by forcing it to fail an Army Courage Test.

Battlefield

The terrain for the battlefield can be chosen in a mutually agreed manner, or randomly determined as laid out in the rules at the start of the Scenarios chapter. Alternatively, the battlefield can be laid out as below, with each side rolling a dice to determine which from which opposing table edge they deploy. On the map below the armies deploy from the North and South table edges.

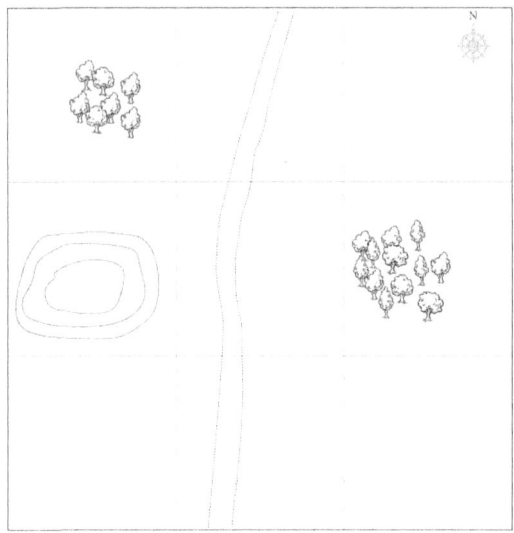

Forces

The forces are equal. Choose two equal forces from the Army Lists chapter or use points values. An Army of between 6 to 8 units would be appropriate.

Deployment

The armies arrive in a piece-meal fashion depending on the order of march. Before deploying both players divide their armies into three divisions and allocate units to each division. Each division must have at least one unit and cannot have more than three units. Each division is numbered 1, 2 or 3. At the start of the battle no units are deployed. At the start of the first Round the player with Priority rolls a d6. A 1-2 indicates that units from division 1 can deploy, 3-4 indicates that division 2 can deploy and 5-6 indicates that division 3 can deploy. The player without Priority does the same during their turn. Deployment is up to each unit's movement allowance from the table edge. Units from the same division must deploy within 12" of each other. The same roll is made in the next two Rounds by each player until all their divisions are deployed. Both armies are eager to come to blows so no divisions may be held back for a later Round.

First Turn

Roll for Priority using the normal rules.

Special Rules

No special rules for this scenario.

Duration of the Battle

Until one or both armies fail an Army Courage Test.

Victory Conditions

An army wins when the opposing army fails an Army Courage Test and they do not. If both armies fail an Army Courage Test the battle is a draw.

Flank Attack

Two armies are jostling for advantage. One army has sent a force on a march to outflank the other. Meanwhile it must hold on as the enemy tries to destroy it while it is weaker. The army with the outflanking force dispatched is Red. The other army is Blue.

Objectives

The objective for both armies is the same, to defeat the other by forcing it to fail an Army Courage Test.

Battlefield

The terrain for the battlefield can be chosen in a mutually agreed manner, or randomly determined as laid out in the rules at the start of the Scenarios chapter. Alternatively, the battlefield can be laid out as below, with each side rolling a dice to determine which from which opposing table edge they deploy. On the map below the armies deploy from the North and South table edges.

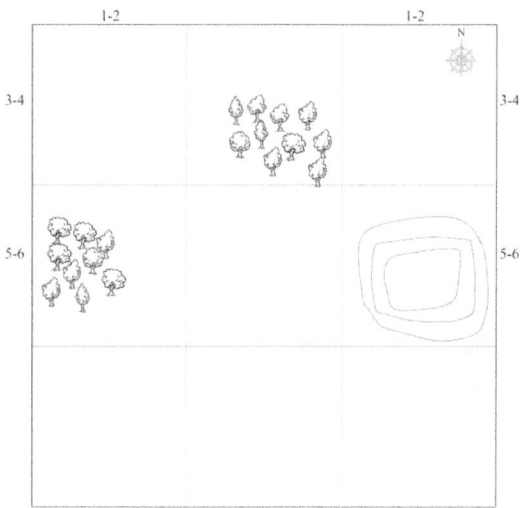

Forces

The forces are equal. Choose two equal forces from the Army Lists chapter or use points values. An Army of between 6 to 8 units would be appropriate.

If the armies are 6 units each, then 2 units from Red's army are off table on the flank march. If armies are 8 units each, then 3 units are conducting the flank march.

Deployment

Blue deploys on the North side of the table and Red deploys on the South. Red deploys all their units not on a flank march first within 6" of the table edge. Blue then deploys within 6" of their table edge.

Red also writes on a piece of paper either West or East to determine which flank their flanking force will arrive on.

First Turn

Blue takes the first turn.

Special Rules

Red does not know how long the flank march will take. Perhaps the flanking force might even get lost and not arrive until after the battle has finished! Every Round after the first roll a dice at the beginning of Blue's turn. On a 5 or 6 the flanking force arrives! Then dice to determine where they arrive. Roll 1d6. On a 1 or 2 they arrive anywhere on the Northern table edge. On 3-4 they arrive at the top third of the nominated table edge. On 5-6 they arrive in the centre third of the nominated Table edge. See Battlefield map above for details.

Duration of the Battle

Until one or both armies fail an Army Courage Test.

Victory Conditions

An army wins when the opposing army fails an Army Courage Test and they do not. If both armies fail an Army Courage Test the battle is a draw.

Last Stand

The Blue army has been defeated in battle and the remains of the King's bodyguard try to protect him from capture by the Red Army.

Objectives

The Blue army is surrounded but in a strong defensive position. The objective for both armies is the same: to survive and force the other army to fail an Army Courage Test. As the Blue army are fighting for their lives, they receive a +1 modifier on any Army Courage Test.

Battlefield

The battlefield is fairly open apart from a hill or walled area in the centre of the battlefield where the Blue Army will make their last stand. A suggested terrain layout is provided below.

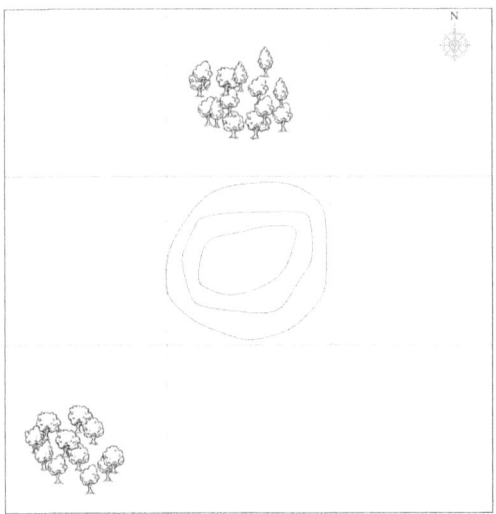

Forces

The Blue Army has 3 units remaining to defend their King. These are the best of the King's household retainers though so can be only Mounted Knights and/or Foot Knights. They can field other units instead if they wish.

The Red Army is 6 units strong, chosen from a standard Army List.

Deployment

The Blue Army deploys first on the hill in the centre of the battlefield. If using your own set-up, then the Blue Army should occupy the central 1-foot square of the battlefield.

Red deploys all their units on any table edge.

First Turn

The Red Army has the first turn.

Special Rules

The Blue Army receive a +1 on any Army Courage Test.

Duration of the Battle

Until one or both armies fail an Army Courage Test.

Victory Conditions

An army wins when the opposing army fails an Army Courage Test and they do not. If both armies fail an Army Courage Test the battle is a draw.

Ambush

The Red Army is marching through the territory of Blue, perhaps on their way back from a raiding expedition. Blue has hidden forces to ambush Red as it passes along a road through dense terrain such as a forest. Blue is heading for a walled town or fortress just to the east and this is the last chance Red has to spring the trap. As Blue approaches the Red army emerges from hiding and attacks.

Objectives

Red's objective is to destroy Blue and cause them to fail an Army Courage Test. Blue's objective is to escape with most of their forces intact by moving their army off the opposite edge.

Battlefield

A table which is longer than it is wider might be a good idea to provide more of a challenge. A layout for a 3'x3' table is provided below, but it would be easy to extend this to 4'x3' for instance. The table should feature a road running West to East and plenty of woods and other terrain from which Red units can emerge to ambush Blue. Although be careful about crowding the table with too many woods as most units are unable to move through them.

Forces

Both armies are equally matched. Choose armies of between 6 and 8 units.

Deployment

Blue is marching along a road from West to East. Blue's units are deployed on the actual road or to either side of it facing from West to East. They can be deployed up to 1' onto the table.

Red deploys their units up to 6" from the Northern and Souther table edges. None are hidden. It is assumed that Blue has spotted the ambushing Red Army and must now get past it to reach the safety of the Eastern table edge.

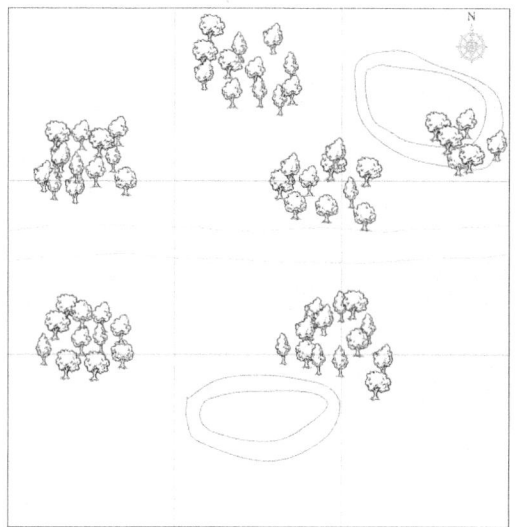

First Turn

Blue takes the first turn.

Special Rules

No special rules apply.

A variation on this scenario might include an additional Blue unit being sent from the walled city or fortress in the East to support them after a certain number of terms. Their arrival could be determined randomly. For instance they appear on the road on the Eastern table edge from Round 4 on a roll of 5 or 6.

Duration of the Battle

Until one or both armies fail an Army Courage Test, or Blue moves three units off the Eastern table edge.

Victory Conditions

Red wins in the standard way by forcing Blue to fail an Army Courage Test. Blue must move at least half of their army off the Eastern table edge.

Rear Guard

The Red army is falling back pursued by Blue. The Red army has left in place a rearguard force to slow the advance of Blue and to allow the rest of their army to escape safely. Blue must defeat the rearguard as soon as possible so that they can continue their pursuit of the main Red army.

Objectives

Red must prevent Blue units from getting past them to pursue the rest of their army. Blue's objective is to destroy the rearguard as quickly as possible and move units past them to pursue Red's main force.

Battlefield

Any set-up would work for this battle, but a suggested set-up including deployment zones is shown below. The battlefield below is an arid rocky landscape.

Forces

The rearguard represents only a portion of Red's forces, while the force belonging to Blue is larger it is not their whole force, some of which are trying to outflank the rearguard via other routes off the battlefield. For a standard sized game Red should have 4 units and Blue should have 6.

Deployment

Red deploys first and may place units anywhere on the battlefield except within 12" of the Eastern table edge. Blue deploys second on the Eastern table edge.

First Turn

Red takes the first turn.

Special Rules

The Red rearguard have promised to die fighting to save the rest of their army. The Red Army receive a +1 on any Army Courage Test.

Duration of the Battle

Red aims to delay the advance of Blue as much as possible. The battle will end after 6 turns.

Victory Conditions

Blue wins by either forcing Red to fail an Army Courage Test and not failing one themselves, or by exiting 3 units off the Western table edge.

Red wins by either forcing Blue to fail an Army Courage Test and not failing one themselves and preventing Blue from exiting 3 units off the Western table edge. All other results are a draw.

River Crossing

A major river divides the territory controlled by both armies. The crossing points are vital to either defend or attack the enemy's territory and must be seized.

Objectives

The objective of both armies is the same: to control the crossings over the river.

Battlefield

A river runs from west to east across the battlefield. There are two fords or bridges along the length of the river approximately 12" in from the western and eastern table edges. Place a few other terrain features but don't crowd the table too much. See below for an example battlefield layout.

Forces

Both armies have an equal number of units from between 6 and 8 units each.

Deployment

Armies deploy on either the Northern or Southern table edge once terrain has been set-up. Roll a dice to determine who deploys on which table edge. Armies can deploy units 6" in from their table edge. Each player rolls a dice to determine who deploys first.

First Turn

Each player rolls a dice to determine who has the first turn.

Special Rules

The river can only be crossed at a ford or bridge, the rest of the river is impassable terrain.

Duration of the Battle

The battle lasts 6 turns or until one or both armies fail an Army Courage Test.

Victory Conditions

If one army has a unit on or across the ford or bridge without an enemy unit engaging them in melee at the end of the game they receive 1 Victory point. The army with more Victory Points at the end of the game is the winner. If the number of Victory points for both players is equal or zero then the game is a draw.

Army Lists

The Army lists presented here are suggested lists for armies of six units each. As the number of units in a game is quite small (between 6 and 8 units usually), it doesn't make sense to come up with a points system and build armies that way as there will always be one army with more and less points than another. All battles are unbalanced and part of the skill of the general is to use their army to the best of their ability to win the glory of victory. The armies in the lists should give a reasonably historical army and a good challenge for most players.

In case the historical unit corresponding to the game unit is not obvious a note is sometimes provided in parentheses - for instance the Foot Knights in the Anglo-Saxon army are intended to be Huscarls.

If you choose 8 units then that can provide more flexibility to choose different units. It is suggested when adding the two additional units you try to be proportional. So for instance for a Crusader army, only one of the additional units should be a Mounted Knight Unit, with the other being perhaps Infantry or Archers.

You can of course change the lists as much as you like. For instance, the Hundred Years War English list is based on the basic split between foot men-at-arms and archers at a battle like Agincourt. But at Poitiers there was also a small contingent of Mounted Knights used so one of the Archers Units could be swapped here for Mounted Knights.

Crusader Army

2 Mounted Knights

1 Light Cavalry (Turcopoles)

2 Archers

1 Infantry

Saracen Army

1 Mounted Knight

2 Light Cavalry

2 Infantry

1 Archer

Normans

2 Mounted Knight

2 Infantry

2 Archers

Anglo-Saxons

2 Foot Knights (Huscarls)

3 Infantry

1 Archers

Feudal Army

3 Mounted Knights

1 Archer

2 Infantry

Scottish Army

1 Mounted Knights

4 Foot Knights (Pike or Close order Spearmen)

1 Archer

Welsh Army

1 Mounted Knight

1 Infantry

2 Archers

2 Light Infantry

Flemish Army

3 Foot Knights (Well motivated urban militia)

2 Infantry (Less well-trained militia)

1 Archer

Hundred Years War English Early

2 Foot Knights or 1 Foot Knight and 1 Mounted Knight

1 Infantry

3 Archers

Hundred Years War English Late

2 Foot Knights

4 Archers

Hundred Years War French

3 Mounted Knights

2 Archers (Crossbows)

1 Infantry

Wars of the Roses Yorkist or Lancastrian

1 Foot Knights

2 Infantry

3 Archers

Swiss Army

4 Foot Knights (Pikemen)

1 Infantry (Halberdiers - less well-armoured)

1 Archer (Crossbows)

Burgundian Army

1 Mounted Knight

1 Foot Knights (Pikemen)

4 Archers (Crossbows and Longbows)

Mongols

2 Mounted Knights

4 Light Cavalry

Rules Summary/Quick Reference Sheet

The game is split into rounds. In each round there are three phases:

- Movement - units can move – half move if crossing difficult terrain, woods, obstacles
- Archery - Light Cavalry and Archers can shoot ranged weapons
- Melee - units engaged in hand-to-hand combat must fight

Units

Unit Name	Move	Archery Hits	Range	Melee Hits	Save	Stamina
Mounted Knights	9"	n/a	n/a	1d6+1/1d6	4+	6
Light Cavalry	12"	1d6-2	12"	1d6-2	6+	6
Foot Knights	4"	n/a	n/a	1d6	3+	6
Infantry	6"	n/a	n/a	1d6-1	4+	6
Archers	6"	1d6-1	18"	1d6-2	5+	6
Light Infantry	9"	n/a	n/a	1d6-2	6+	6
General	12"	n/a	n/a	+1	n/a	n/a

Archery Procedure

Roll modified 1d6 for Hits.
Target then rolls to Save each Hit.
If Target in cover then +1 to Save.
Each unsaved Hit results in one lost point of Stamina.

When stamina is 0 unit will need to make Unit Courage Test.

Melee Procedure

As per Archery but all units engaged roll to Hit. If engaged by multiple enemies, unit must split Hits between them.

Modifiers to Hit:

+1 if Uphill
+1 if Enemy Recoiled in the last Round
+1 if General is with the Unit

Modifier to Save:

+1 if Infantry and Foot Knights flanked by other Infantry or Foot Knights

Unit Courage Test

If Stamina 0 make Unit Courage Test on 2d6. 7 or less OK, 8 or more Unit breaks and is removed from table.

Army Courage Test

If half or more Units lost make Army Courage Test. 8 or less to succeed (6 or less if General dead or captured). If fail, then Army breaks.

Generals

+1 to Melee Hits, +1 to Unit Courage Test. Can remove 3 Hits from Unit once in a battle.

Printed in Dunstable, United Kingdom